Instant Needlepoint Designs

By Barbara Fields and Lorelle Phillips
Illustrated By Carol Nicklaus

GROSSET & DUNLAP c 1973
Publishers   New York

ISBN: 0-448-01312-6 (hardbound)
ISBN: 0-448-11617-0 (paperbound)

First Printing

Printed in the United States of America

Contents

Introduction

Up to now, needlepoint design has been an involved and expensive process. This book is intended to simplify that process by providing the needlepointer with original and beautiful designs that are both economical and easy to transfer onto canvas.

These designs have been created specifically for needlepointing. They are all full size and ready to be traced onto canvas. All are suitable for pillows, but many are also ideal for pocket-books, seat cushions, wall hangings or rugs. Personal touches can be added by altering a color scheme, enlarging a design, working a border, or using any ideas you might have to make our designs become yours.

The directions follow; gather your materials and you are ready to begin. We hope you enjoy needlepointing our designs as much as we have enjoyed creating them.

DIRECTIONS

Materials: Design
Canvas
Waterproof marking pen
Ruler
Flat surface
Good light

Any table or desk is a good surface and any overhead light will do, but a high-intensity bulb is especially helpful. Make sure the pen is waterproof to prevent the color from bleeding onto the wool when the canvas is blocked. We suggest using a light-colored pen for outlining, since a dark pen sometimes shows through the light wool. The ruler will be used only as a guide for some geometric patterns and to outline the borders of your design.

Either single- or double-mesh canvas can be used for these designs. We prefer the single-mesh, or mono, canvas simply because it is easier to see the design as you trace, and the completed picture looks more appealing. This is the reason why most of the designs you see at needlepoint shops are traced onto single-mesh canvas. You can use double-mesh or penelope canvas if you prefer, but it is not necessary for any of our designs, and using it might make tracing more difficult.

Both kinds of canvas are measured in squares to the inch: a No. 12 canvas has 12 squares to the inch, a No. 13, 13 squares to the inch, etc. With each design, we have indicated the size mesh we think should be used. Usually there is more than one choice. The amount of detail in the design and the particular look you are trying to achieve will determine the gauge you choose. Generally, the more intricate patterns should be done on canvas that has no less than 12 squares to an inch. Sometimes an even smaller mesh might be needed. The larger gauge is more effective if you are trying to achieve a bold or textured quality, and, of course, the bigger the mesh size, the larger the stitches and the faster the piece will be finished. We advise a beginner to choose a design that can be stitched on a No. 10 or gros point canvas. As you acquire skills, or if you already have some facility, don't hesitate to try a more complex design. Working with fine line and detail can be a rewarding and creative experience.

Once you have decided on the gauge you wish to use, buy a canvas that measures at least two inches larger on all sides than the design you are going to trace. Then tape the edges to prevent fraying.

Tracing the Design

Study the design until you are familiar with it. Then center the canvas over the design in the book. Take your pen and trace the design lightly so a fine line is achieved. There is no need to pin or tape the canvas and the design together. Just hold them firmly with one hand as you begin to trace, and follow the pattern. If the canvas slips or if you want to inspect the design, you can lift the canvas and replace it exactly by using the part of the design you've already traced as your guide.

When a pattern or design is symmetrical, watch the straight lines or diagonals to be sure you are following along the proper row. It is very easy to follow the lines on a canvas, whether they are vertical, horizontal or diagonal. If you make a mistake in the tracing and the pen slips to another row, you can correct it easily as you stitch. Make sure, too, that the hole count is even on both sides. This simply means that when you work with a symmetrical design, stitch one side exactly the same as the other, covering the same number of squares (holes) on both sides of the canvas.

Where the detail seems too small to trace, copy it with a pencil directly on the canvas. Don't worry if the detail is not exactly like ours; the effect achieved will be the same.

How to Work With Graphed Designs

Some geometrical and symmetrical designs are difficult to line up evenly on the canvas no matter how carefully you trace them. We have decided to graph these designs along with portions of a few repeat patterns. They are not to be traced. Transferring a design from graph paper to your canvas involves another process.

Begin two inches from the top and side of the canvas—or in the center if indicated in a particular design. Pretend that the canvas is your graph and simply copy the stitch pattern onto it. For instance, on a graphed design you might see five squares in one color and two in another. Fill in the same five squares in one color on your canvas and then the other two and so on. Where the design is black and white, imagine that the white or black squares are also a color.

All our graphs are on 10-to-the-inch graph paper. You can use larger- or smaller-mesh canvas if you wish. Again, remember that if you use a mesh bigger than that on the graph, the finished piece will be slightly larger and more coarsely textured. The opposite will be true if the canvas gauge is smaller than that of the graph.

Correcting a Traced Design

If you should happen to make a mistake there is a simple procedure to follow. Buy a tube of white *acrylic* paint, squeeze it into a dish and thin it with a little water so it won't clog the holes in your canvas. Take a thin watercolor brush, dip into the paint and paint out your mistake. If the holes should get clogged, a toothpick will clean them out.

Color Coding a Canvas

Since it is easier to carry a traced canvas than an entire book, we suggest color coding your design before buying the yarn. If you mark the wool number or paint a small amount of color in each section of the design, it will facilitate both choosing the color and deciding how much wool you actually need. If the colors are all dark, you can use magic markers. If they are light, remember to use only oil or acrylic paint to prevent bleeding onto the wool when the finished piece is blocked.

Wool

The colors in our designs are keyed to Persian Yarn, manufactured by Paternayan Bros. and found in most needlepoint, yarn and department stores. The colors range from the most vibrant tone of a shade to the palest of its hues, and the variations are limitless. The actual yarn colors may not exactly match the printed colors, as it is impossible to achieve exact matching with printer's inks. If you choose to work with another brand of yarn, use our color descriptions as a guide.

The yarn comes three-ply, which means that three strands of yarn are twisted together. This thickness is fine for a 10-mesh canvas. Sometimes, however, the three-ply is too heavy for the gauge you have chosen. As the mesh size of the canvas becomes smaller, the number of threads you use will be less. In general, while the No. 10 canvas takes a three-ply, Nos. 12, 13 and 14 will take two-ply. Very small mesh canvases take only one-ply. Gros point mesh needs two three-ply worked together or the special yarn that is made specifically for gros point canvas.

As a rule, if the wool seems too tight or the stitches do not line up easily, take out one of the plys by unwinding it from the others and work one less strand.

How Much Wool to Buy

This question always seems a mystery to the beginning needlepointer, but there is an easy solution. Bring the design either in the book or on the canvas to the store where you will buy your supplies for needlepoint. They are experts at it and will be glad to tell you how much wool you need.

How to Start a Needlepoint

Once you have traced your design and bought your wool you are ready to begin needlepointing. It is usually best to start in the center of a design and work toward the edges.

Thread a needle suitable for the thickness of the yarn and begin your first stitch by holding an inch or two of the yarn behind the canvas, covering it with your next stitches as you work. Successive threads are both begun and finished by weaving them into already existing yarn on the back of the canvas. Never knot the wool. Weaving it will hold it firmly in place.

The continental stitch is the most common of the needlepoint stitches and can be worked on all the designs in this book. Other stitches may be used as desired but remember the primary rule of needlepoint: every stitch on a canvas must always be worked in the same direction. If you are a beginning needlepointer any one of the following books might be helpful.

1. *Needlepoint* by Hope Hanley, Charles Scribner's Sons
2. *Needlepoint for Everyone* by Mary Brooks Picken and Doris White, Harper & Row
3. *Do it Yourself Needlepoint*, Joan Scobey and Lee Par McGrath, Essandess Special Editions, Simon and Schuster
4. *Needlepoint Design* by Louis Gartner, Jr., William Morrow & Co.

Enlarging a Design

All of our designs can be enlarged by placing them on a larger background or by adding borders. However, if the design you like is too small for a specific project you might want to enlarge the picture itself. The simplest method is to have the design photostated. Bring the design (the book or a tracing) to a camera shop or photostater. They can enlarge it to any size in a day or two.

You can also enlarge a design by using a grid. Take a piece of paper a little larger than your planned project. Using a T square or drawing triangle, outline the borders of the design. Divide the space into squares. Then take the original design and divide it into the same number of squares. You can then copy the design square by square onto the larger paper.

Finishing Your Canvas

Needlepoint canvas changes its shape so much as it is sewn that a beginning needlepointer can become quite alarmed at its appearance. Blocking sets the canvas back to its original shape.

Many people are apprehensive about blocking and finishing a canvas themselves and take their needlework to a professional who will block it and put it into finished form. If the finished piece is large or intended for upholstery or a rug, we strongly suggest that you have it done professionally. Any upholsterer will do it for you and will make pillows of any size or shape as well.

If you decide to have a pillow blocked and made professionally be sure to discuss the type of

filling and the shape because it does make a difference in the price. A dacron filler will cost about $13 in a twelve-inch-square finished pillow while a down filler might add on another $8 or more. A down-filled pillow is soft and pliable while the dacron is firmer but there is no other difference between the two. The shape of the pillow can also affect the price. A single-edged pillow is much less expensive than one made with gussets.

Some needlepointers enjoy doing their own blocking and finishing, particularly if they are making their design into a pillow. It is an ambitious task but rewarding to work a needlepoint project through from the first tracing to the final product.

To do this you will need a board larger than the needlepoint, brown paper, rustproof tacks, a piece of lining or a cloth diaper and an iron.

Before you begin to trace, measure the design in the book. If you are going to add a border, measure that and add it to the size of the illustration. Then cut a pattern out of heavy brown paper that is about two inches larger all around than the design itself. Outline the size of the design on the paper pattern.

Tack the paper to the board. Wet the lining or diaper and lay it on top of your finished needlepoint. Set your iron at high, and with the steam off, press the material until the needlepoint is quite damp. You might have to wet the material a few times before the needlepoint is damp enough to stretch into shape.

Fit the needlepoint onto the paper and tack it down about every half inch, stretching it to fit the pattern. Remember to use only rustproof tacks and to tack on the surrounding canvas, not on the design. Then leave it for at least twenty-four hours or until it is completely dry. Sometimes this process must be repeated several times before the canvas will hold its original shape.

When the blocking is completed, the needlepoint can be made into its intended form.

How to Make a Pillow

Any fairly heavy material, including a coarse cotton, is good backing. Whether you use welting or not, be sure to sew the material as close to the stitches as possible. Some people even include the last row or two of the needlepoint stitches to make certain that no unfinished canvas will show. . When three sides are done, trim the excess canvas, insert your filler and finish the remaining side. If you add a zipper you will be able to take out the filler and dry clean the pillowslip.

How to Make a Belt

To fashion a belt from your finished needlepoint it is necessary to cut down the two-inch selvage around the edges to one inch or less. Remember it must be wide enough to fold under the lining that will cover the inside of the belt. The lining can be made of any suitable material but grosgrain ribbon is the easiest since it has body and is finished on the edges. Pin the belt to the ribbon, folding down the selvage to the edge of the stitched canvas.

If you are going to use a buckle, make the belt a little longer so you will have enough to sew around the shaft. If you don't have a special buckle, before sewing the lining, braid the strands of yarn in the colors of your design, knotting them on one end, and pull them them through each end of the canvas, to be tied together for a fastening.

Designs

Peony

Don't be intimidated by the complexity of this beautiful design. It is really one of the easiest to trace. A 14-gauge canvas suits it perfectly, its small mesh enhancing the delicacy of the flowering forms.

The separate petals, leaves and buds can be outlined either in a single color or combination of colors. You might outline each leaf in a shade or two deeper than the leaf itself. This would lend a subtle and fluid quality to the design while a bolder one-color outline would add definition to each shape.

The reason we so strongly suggest outlining is because this design tends to float on the background and needs to be anchored in some way. If you don't want to outline completely, then use a very dark background and outline only those shapes that need to be differentiated from those surrounding them.

Colors
Background 644, pink petals 281, green leaves 510, chartreuse shading 550, gray shading 184, redpink center 821, orange 424, yellow shading 447

Lazy Pandas

These tired pandas make an enjoyable project for the beginning needlepointer. They are meant to be worked in two colors and would make a charming pillow for a child's room. The most important areas to watch are the spaces between the two pandas and the pattern of their faces. Once this is done, these comic characters will come to life.

Colors
We suggest the black and white of the design with a background color of your choice.

Strawberry Warbler

The classical elegance of this design requires an expert hand. Careful tracing is critically important. If you find the detail overwhelming, feel free to omit some of the strawberries or perhaps some of the leaves. You will still be left with the bird on the branch, framed by the ribbon. With the addition of the year or a name this design is appropriate as a commemorative gift. A No. 14 canvas must be used if you wish to achieve the delicacy you see in the drawing.

Colors
Strawberries, border ribbon and butterfly 639, 821, bird 773, pink breast 288, gray 137, beak, butterfly, flowers Y44, blue in branch 355, branch 443, feet 457, butterfly body Y40, leaves 545, inside 565, darker leaves G54

Repeating Shell Pattern

Opposite

This is probably one of the easiest and most interesting repeat designs that a needlepointer can do. The size and color possibilities are endless. The finished piece can cover a chair, a couch, a piano stool, or it can be a rug. It's hard to imagine where this design could not be used with tremendous effect.

The shells can be worked in two colors, three colors, four or as many as you choose. Alternate or diagonal rows could be different colors. Your imagination can really have free reign.

We have graphed a section of the design and we suggest that you do not trace this one. Once you count out the graphed section and start copying the design you will be able to complete it easily.

There is no "right side up" in this design. The shells can face up or down. Any size canvas is appropriate.

Colors

Shell outlines: dark moss green 505; flower shapes: bright rose 821; shell background: bright yellow Y44; curved lines: burnt orange 424

Cherries on Plaid

Page 22

Trace the cherries first, then the surrounding plaid. You don't even have to trace the entire plaid, just enough to indicate the length and width of each line. You will be able to continue along the proper rows as you stitch. Work the design in the same manner, beginning in the center with the cherries, then progressing to the plaid.

We suggest that the thinner bands of plaid cover two squares on your canvas and the thicker bands four squares. The spaces between the plaid bands that are not part of the background should be five squares each. However, the lines of the plaid can be any thickness you wish.

This design can be expanded to any size by extending the plaid to the length and width your project calls for. This might be done for a piano bench or a window seat.

A beginner might like to try this design in gros point.

Colors

Cherries 845, 639, leaves G54, 550, red plaid 242, yellow Y44, aqua 773, purple 643, little orange square 968

Sarah, Lisa, and Kate

Page 23

There is no reason why a novice needlepointer could not try this charming design. The large areas of background broken by the rhythmic placement of the three Victorian girls make it both easy and interesting to work. Our choice of colors emphasizes the turn-of-the-century theme; should you decide to change them, keep this in mind. To capture the fine line of this illustration, use a 12-gauge canvas.

Colors

Blue sky 741, yellow hats 457, green grass 574, dark bushes 545, light bushes and dress 565, cinnamon hair 424, yellow hair 441, gold hair, shoes, tennis racquet 447, green hat decoration G64, red apple and shuttlecock R10, gray stockings 137, skin 831, pink dress 828, dark brown shoes 247, aqua dress 793

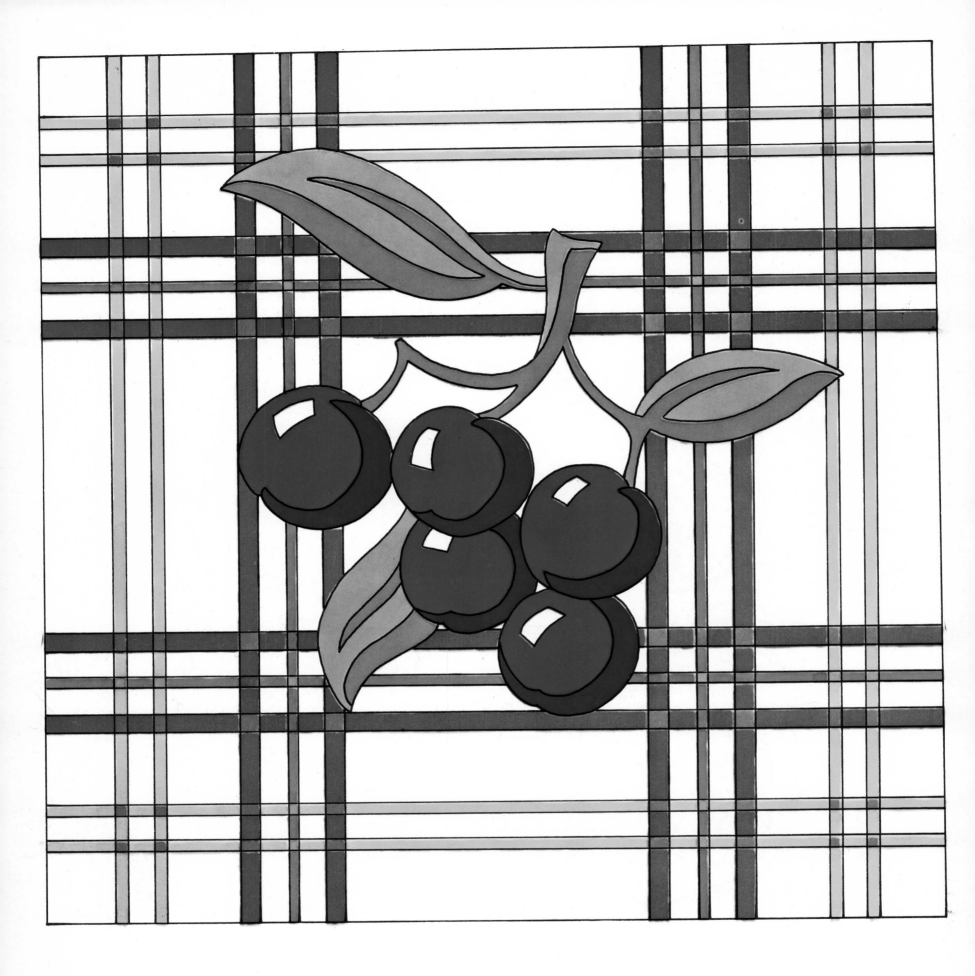

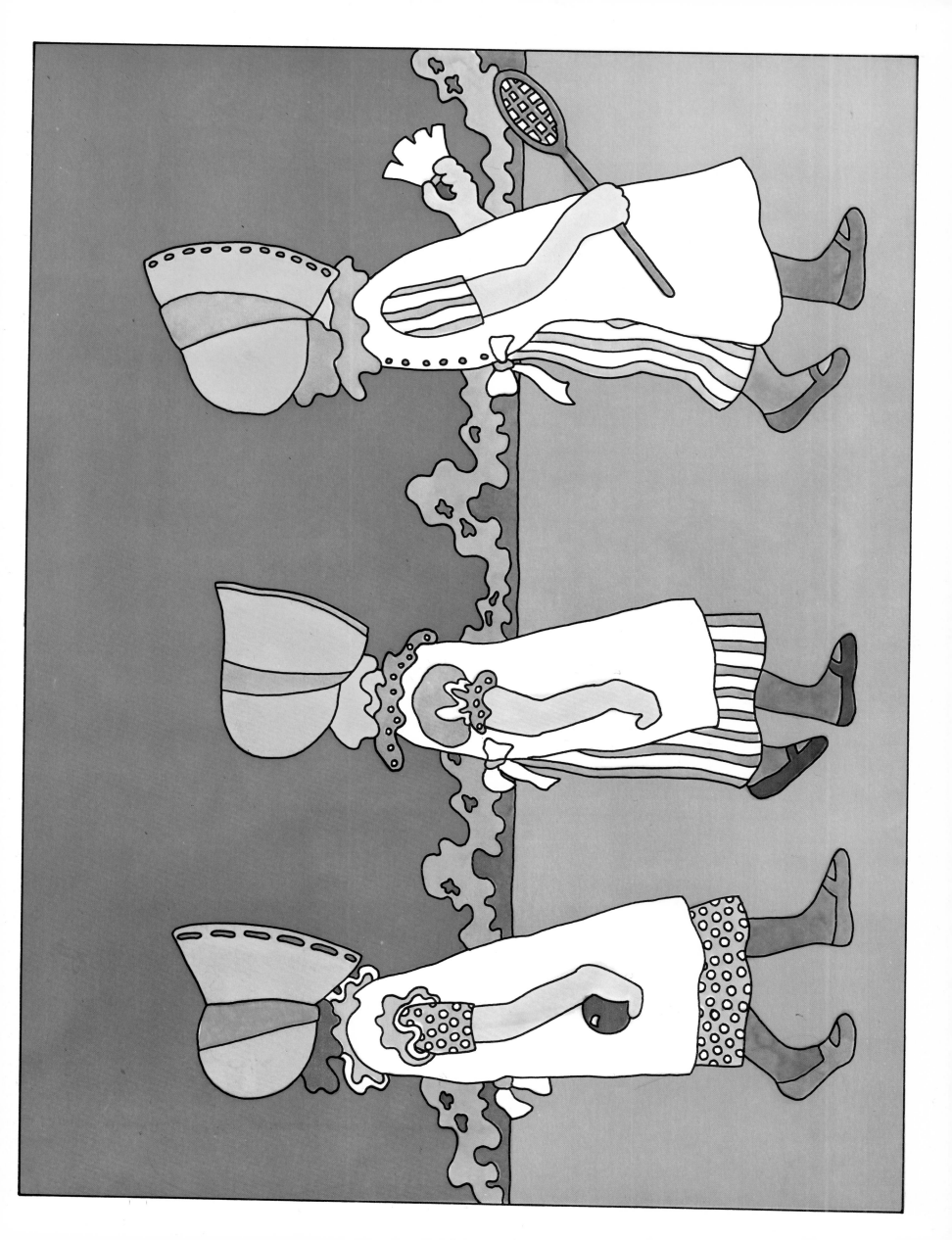

Three Turkish Emblems

Since only half of these designs are printed, remember when buying canvas that each design will be twice the size. They are printed on graph paper and are quite simple to transfer to any gauge canvas. Each design must be counted out, but the designs are not complicated, and since there is little detail the counting will be easy. These patterns could be fashioned into a beautiful rug, separately or together. Use as many squares as you need, sewing them together to achieve the desired size.

Opposite: Turkish Emblem Number 1
Colors
Background: maroon 231; center arrow: blue 355; first border outline: yellow 441; jagged cross border: jade 591; two horns: red R74; shading of horn: white

Page 26: Turkish Emblem Number 2
Colors
Blue background 773, gold Y40, green G54, fuchsia 645, pink 829, dark fuchsia 639

Page 27: Turkish Emblem Number 3
Colors
Center motif: dusky blue 355; background of center motif, umbrella design, quotation mark design under umbrella (facing toward center): white; middle of center motif: burnt rose red R69; exact center of design and background: bright green G54; two large medallions, two small medallions: bright yellow Y44; inside of medallions: magenta 821; large quotation mark: rose red R74

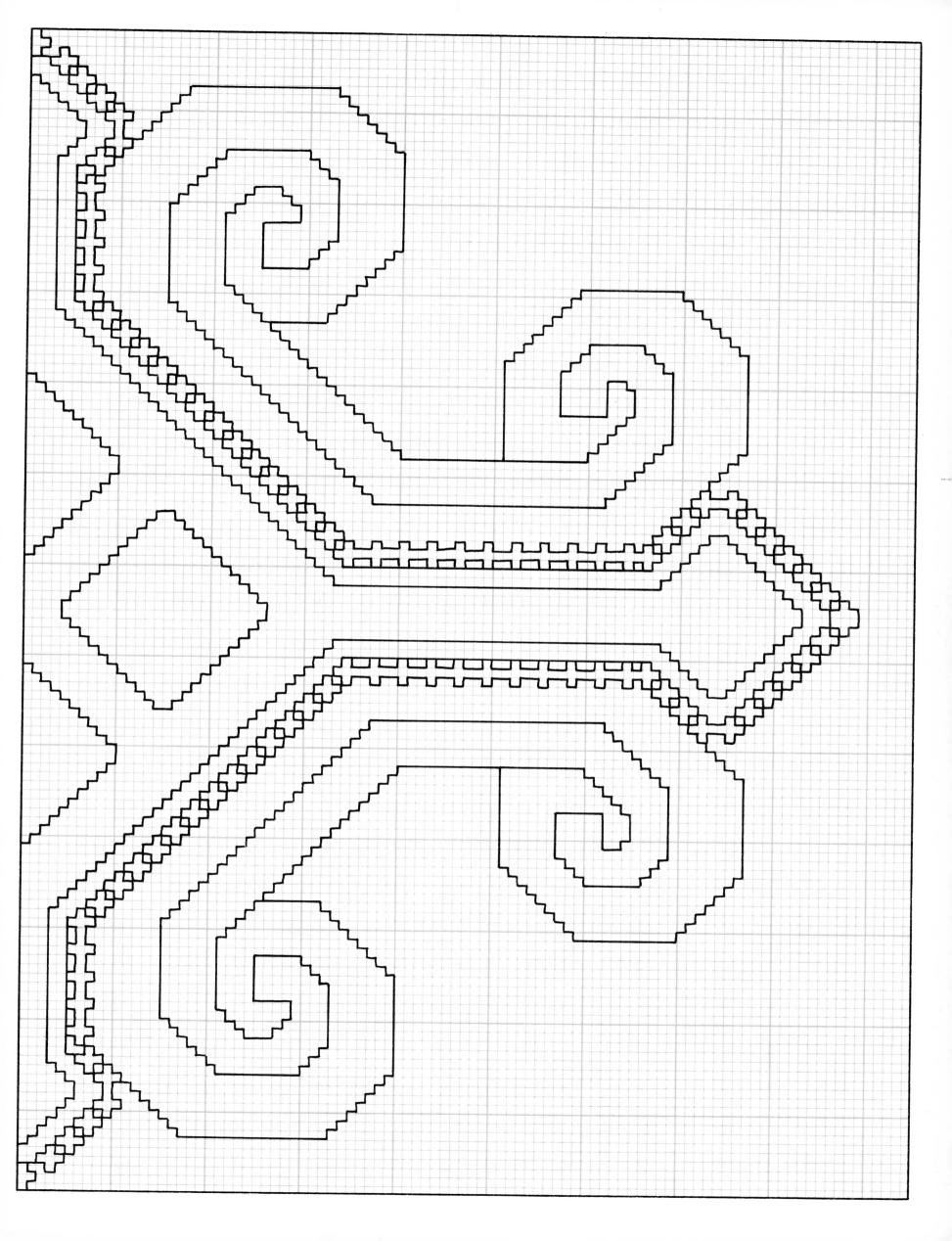

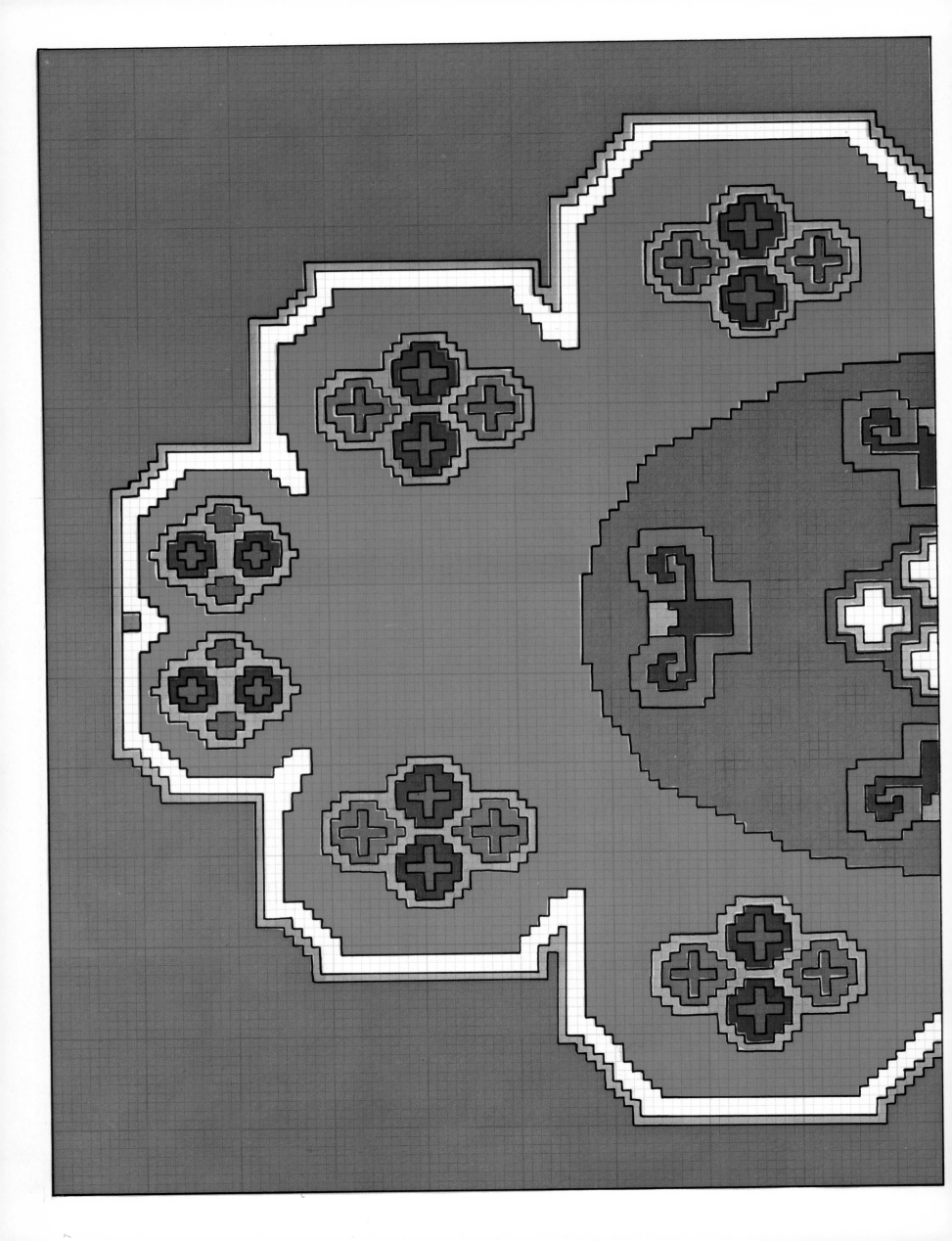

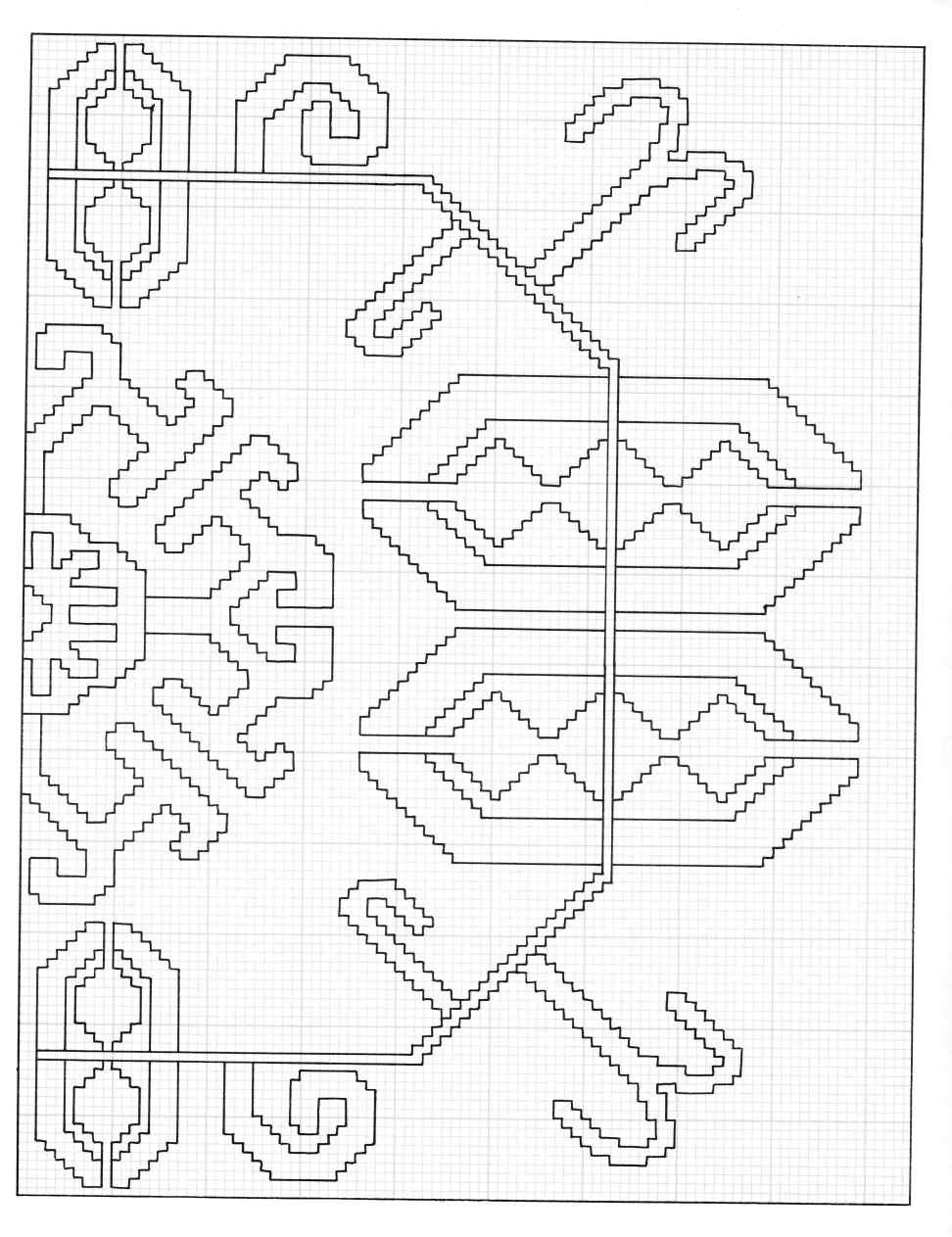

Black and White Flowers

Both geometric and free-flowing, this design combines pattern and line most decoratively. It can be stitched in black and white or any two-color scheme you wish to use. More subtle gradations of color can be achieved by using different hues of a single shade—for instance, three or four tones of blue or rose in chromatic progression.

Trace only a few of the geometrics. The rest can be counted after you do one or two.

A 10-gauge canvas is most suitable to the design, and a beginner or intermediate needle-pointer will enjoy bringing it to life.

Colors
Shaded flowers: shades of slate blue 334, 330, 385, 386, 395; rims of spoke flower: deep red 845; spoke flower: dark pink 850; spokes of flower: pink 860; dark squares: slate blue 334; light squares and background: white; center squares: lighter slate blue 395

Royal Baking Powder

The use of commercial labels as pop art has become very popular in recent years. This striking label, enlarged for needlepoint, incorporates several facets of color and design. The lettering, shadowing and ribbon work, along with the juxtaposition of two primary colors, make this an exciting and challenging piece to work. Because of the lettering, this must be stitched on 12-gauge canvas.

Colors
Red R240, yellow Y42, blue 793, dark shading 311

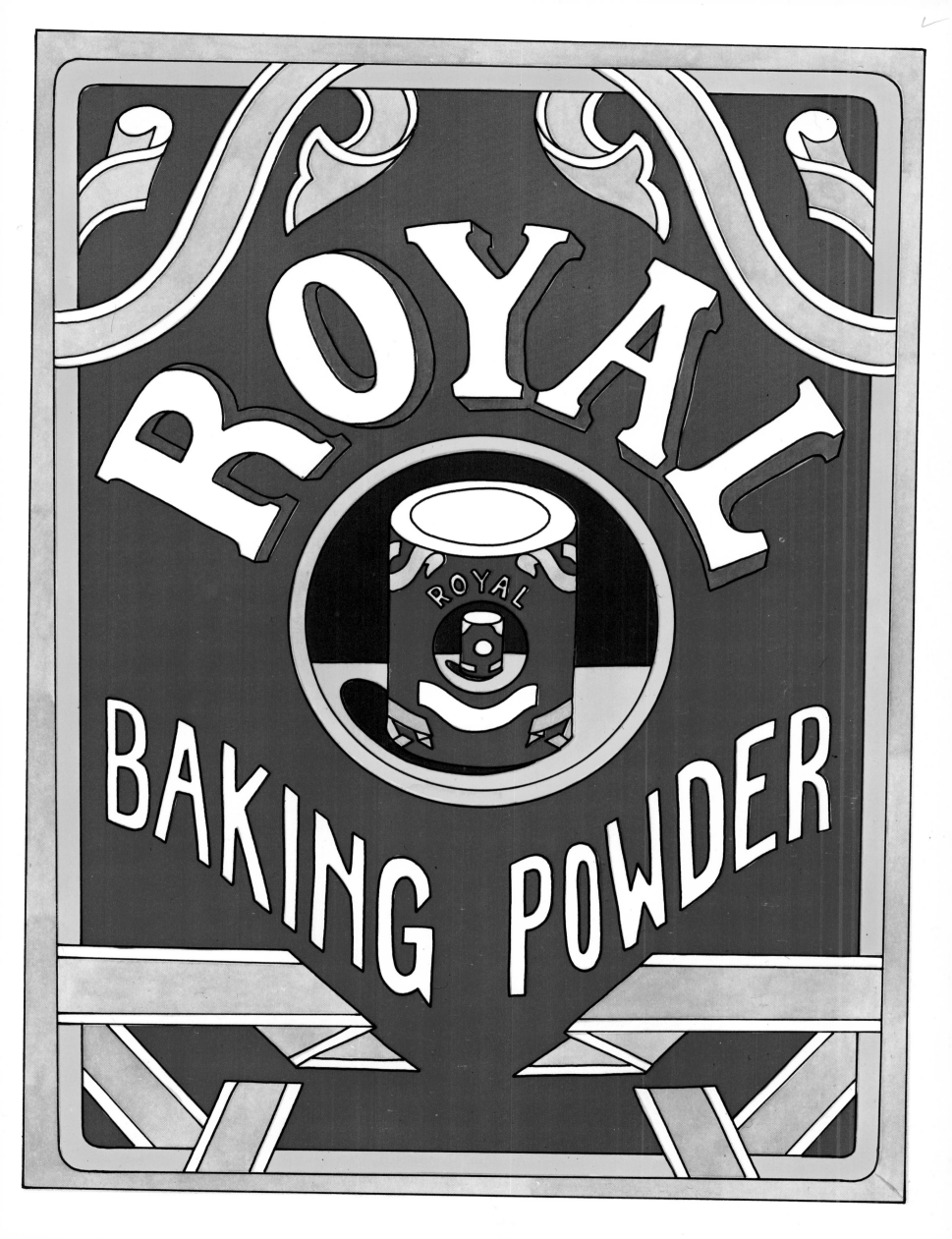

Impressionist Flower

This variegated flower is adaptable to a pillow or cushion. Its flowing quality makes it work equally well in the most informal or formal of rooms. The needlepointing should not be difficult since there are large areas of solid color and the detail is fairly well defined. Because it has fine, rhythmic line, it is most successfully needlepointed on small-gauge canvas.

Colors
Green 553, orange red 843, pink 855, deep brick 242, gold 427, fuchsia 645, chartreuse in tree 550, duller green in tree 555, brighter green in trees G64

Farmer Boy

Opposite

A good beginning design for a young boy. He might have fun making the doll into a puppet by finishing it without a filler and leaving the bottom open.

Colors
Hat, pants: bright yellow Y44; shirt, buttons, some strands of hair and some patches: burnt red 242; other strands of hair: burnt orange 424; patch on hat: light fuchsia 645; skin tone: medium pink 288; cheeks and nose: medium burnt red 843; shoes, neckerchief, some patches: aqua 773; laces and polka dots: white

Flower Girl

Page 36

Our Flower Girl is an ideal companion for any child. It can be stitched as a doll, wall hanging or pillow, separately or together with Farmer Boy. An older child might like to make a doll herself. Use gros point canvas, back it with brightly colored felt or sturdy gingham and stitch up a friend.

Colors
Yellow hat Y44, skin tone 288, dark orange in hair and flowers 424, light orange in hair Y40, purple flower in hat 645, cheek circle and nose 843, flowers 242, 843, 645, 424, greens in leaves G64, 574, G74, turquoise 773, red check 242, basket 419

Bathers

Page 37

These fanciful bathers are both easy to trace and to stitch, making this a wonderful project for a beginner. The only decision to be made is whether or not to outline the figures, and this will depend on the skin tone you choose. If you decide on a light skin tone, the sand and skin colors will be nearly the same, and an outline will probably be necessary. The darker you make the skin, the less need there will be for an outline. Of course, the sand could be grass, and then even lightly colored figures would stand out against the background. Whether you choose sand or grass, try mixing a few shades of one color for a dappled effect.

Colors
Background 975, sky, heart and lady's cheeks 645, umbrellas 311, sun Y40, lady's body 433, man's body and lady's hair 424, hats, bodice, stars and lady's toenails R10, blue in lady and man's shading 350, man's bathing suit 639-569

Folk Scene

The advanced needlepointer will enjoy this design. Its line and detail make it especially interesting, and it will be an attractive accessory for any room. A 12-gauge or smaller canvas is suggested; otherwise the detail is liable to get lost in the translation from design to canvas.

Colors
Outer border: aqua 342; inner border: blue 723; background: yellow Y44; buildings, horse, man's pants, shoes and flower accents: brown 145; saddle, building decorations, grounds and hat: blue 723 and aqua 342; robe, hill outline and bridle: blue 723; leaves: green 555

Magenta and Green Plaid

This symmetrical design is very easy because it employs only verticals and horizontals. It would be an excellent piece for the needlepointer who has never done a geometric before. You will discover quickly that you must only count the width and length of each color and follow it through for the rest of the design. This motif could be repeated ad infinitum so it is especially suitable for a long cushion or even as a rug. Use the colors as we show them or change to ones that fit better into your own color scheme. The canvas size is up to you; you can use gros point or mesh as small as 10 or 12 depending on how delicate you want the finished product to look.

Colors
Magenta 644, orange 434, yellow Y44, red 242, green 510

Earth Banner

A breakaway from traditional needlepoint decoration, this canvas is suitable for a framed wall hanging in any contemporary setting.

Obviously this lends itself to the ecologically minded. It would make a terrific pillow or carry-all bag. If you decide on the bag, an interesting idea for the reverse side would be to trace only the border and the banner, leaving out the words "God Bless Our Home" and replacing it with your name or initials. It is an easy design but must be worked on a small-gauge canvas.

Colors
Background: pale blue 781; water: medium blue 741; earth, palm tree and bush shading: bright green G54; fir trees, bushes, land under palm and earth edge: moss green 505; trunk of palm: brown 201; waves: deep blue 721; sails of boat, sun and outline of banner: bright yellow Y44; boat, flowers and banner: red 242; clouds, moon, stars and lettering: white

God Bless Our Home

Peruvian Dragon

We suggest this vivid design for the needle-pointer who has some experience but who has not tried our method of tracing. It is important to keep the canvas firmly over the design so that the small symbols are placed properly in relation to the dragon.

For the most effective results, use a 12-gauge canvas.

Colors
Orange 965, red R10, fuchsia bird 644, green dragon 545, pinks 649, scales 443

Artichoke

This is one of the easier designs in the book but an enthusiastic beginner will appreciate the challenge of the lettering. It is an obvious choice for a wall hanging or pillow in a kitchen or breakfast room.

Trace it on a No. 10 canvas. Although it looks more appropriate for a gros point, there is just enough detail in both the artichoke and the lettering to warrant a smaller mesh.

The artichoke should be worked in two shades of green, one for the borders of the leaves and one for the leaves themselves. The rest of the colors will be easy to choose if you wish to differ from ours. Once the greens are decided, the others can be made to match both those in the vegetable and in the room where the needlepoint will be.

Colors
Artichoke and frame: green 520; artichoke highlights: lighter green 527; background of artichoke and banner outline: bright orange 960; banner: brown 205; lettering and background of entire design: gold 447

ARTICHOKE

Turkish Pomegranates

Opposite

Taken as a whole, this design would make a charming pillow or wall hanging, effective even when worked only in two colors, one for the design and one for the background. It is also one of those designs that can be enlarged ad infinitum simply by working the design to the length and width you desire. The leaves on the top may be omitted, carrying the shell design throughout the canvas, or you might repeat the shells and the leaves as many times as you like.

Another possibility, particularly useful for a rug, would be to use the entire design as half of the finished piece. Then turn the canvas around and repeat. Finally, separate parts of the design can also be used. For instance, either border would make a handsome belt or could be utilized as a border for another design. And of course, the repeat may be worked as a whole without the borders.

Colors
Rust 424, green 510, yellow Y44, blue 773, hot pink 821

Sectional

Page 50

If you are at all hesitant about tracing your first needlepoint, try this Mondrian-inspired design, as it is very simple to trace. There are only a few words of guidance. Make sure that all your vertical and horizontal lines follow along a straight row on the canvas. As you are tracing, you might find that the marker slips over to another row but

don't worry. While you are needlepointing you will be able to keep within the prescribed squares.

The color combinations are infinite. The design can be done in shades of all one color or you can use the colors in the room where the finished canvas will be. You can choose from a wide range of canvas sizes as well.

Colors
All dark aquas 773, pale aquas 793, red R10, fuchsia 639, green G54, yellow Y44, orange 968

My Hero

Page 51

Work this easy and entertaining design on a No. 10, 12 or 14 canvas, depending on how much detail you desire.

The top of the sandwich can be stitched in a single color with darker or lighter highlights. It might be more challenging, however, to experiment with shading or to split your yarn and twine

two or three tones of a color together to give a slightly textured effect.

The colors of the meats and vegetables can be shaded. Some variation would make it more interesting to stitch and add depth to the detail.

Cheerful and fun, My Hero will give the needlepointer nearly as much pleasure as the real thing.

Colors
Brown bread 419, yellow buttery creases and butter bottom 467, edge of bread and bottom layer 457, light green lettuce 550, dark green edge G64, edge of tomato R69, red inside and edge of bologna 843, pie shapes on tomato, lettering, edge of cheese and pimento 968, cheese 434, bologna and mortadella spots 855, mortadella edge 283, mortadella 447, yellow on banner Y44, fuchsia 645, olive 555

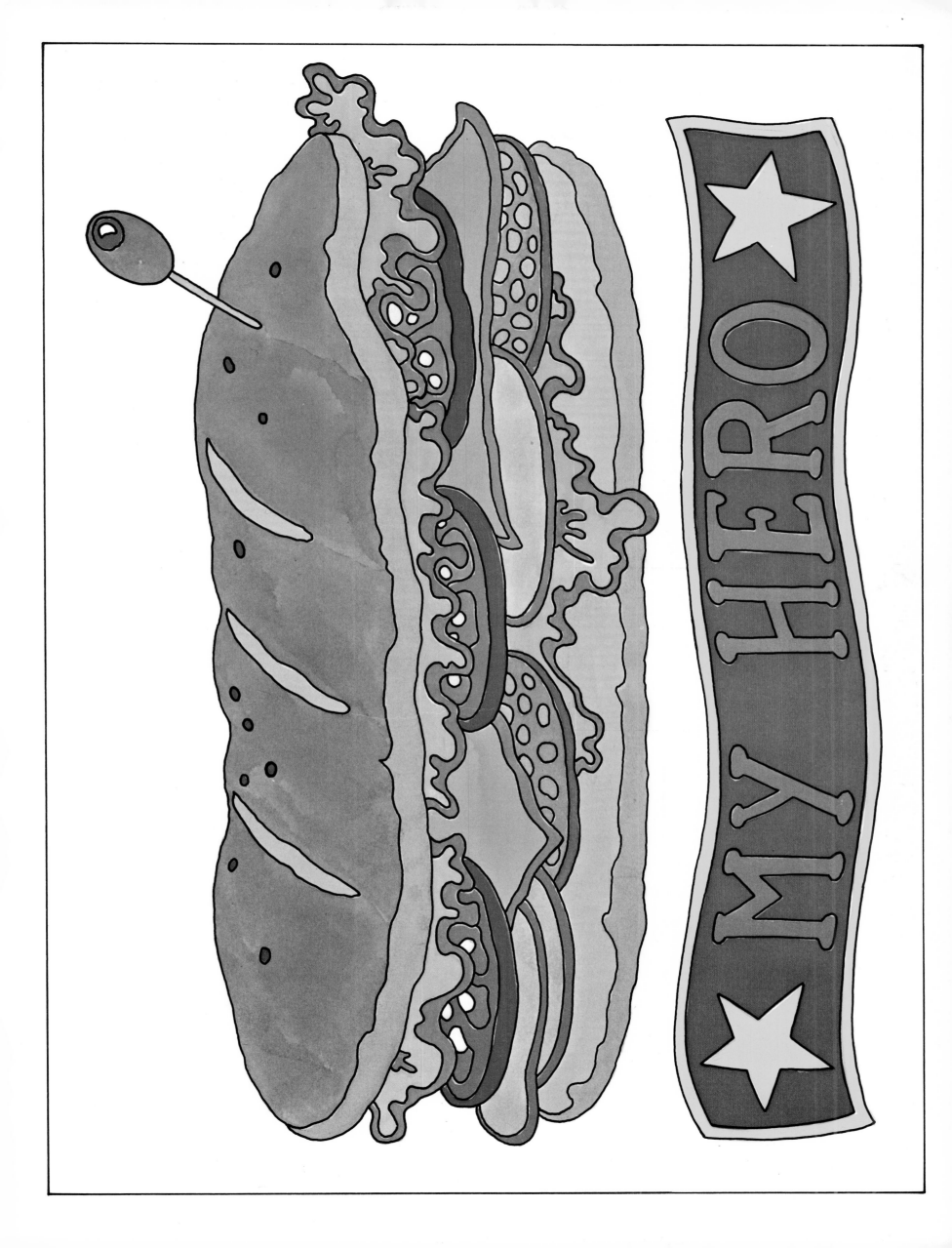

Gingham Flower

Opposite

What could be a prettier combination than gingham and flowers? A set of chair cushions or a group of pillows, each with the gingham in another color scheme, would brighten a kitchen, breakfast room, bedroom or an entire summer house.

Gingham can be stitched in any colors, giving it great versatility as a decorating device. To work a gingham pattern you need two tones of one color—for example, a dark and light red—plus white. Make sure that the contrast between the shades is strong enough to differentiate them from each other. Follow our shading so the darker squares will be your darker shade, the lighter tones your lighter shade, and so on.

A gros point canvas works up well if you decide to use only the gingham, leaving out the flowers. Otherwise, a 12-gauge canvas is necessary.

Colors
Dark gingham squares: bright red R10; light squares: lighter red R70 and white; flowers: combinations of reds R10, R50, R60 and R70; flower accents: yellow Y44; leaves and stems: moss greens 555 and 505

Patchwork Circle

Page 54

This handsome design might look bright on a background of gray or black, bordered by the color checks that are in the design itself.

It can be worked on any gauge but a large mesh will bring out its bold and vivid quality.

Colors
Yellow Y44, blue 718, pink red 821, brick red 242, orange 960, wine 227, green 553

Snowy Landscape

Page 55

We like this design for either a Christmas or New Year's commemorative because of its wintry, peaceful mood. With the addition of the date, the needlepointer's initials and the initials of the person to whom it will be given, it becomes a wonderfully personalized gift. It is not a difficult design and could be done by anyone. Twelve-gauge canvas or smaller will give the most painterly effect for the scene. The numbers and letters (if you decide to use them) work best in a small-gauge canvas.

Colors
Frame and door G54, orange 424, pink 821, sky 733, window and moon 457, tree 510, little tree 505, blue shadowing 330, brown trunk 511, gray shadows 389, brown house 154, chimney 405

Pennsylvania Dutch

This winsome design makes a loving remembrance for a baby or young child. If you wish, a name and date can easily be included in a border.

Trace the bird first. Then trace the hearts lightly. Be sure to begin the needlepoint the same way, by working the bird before you begin the hearts. Don't depend on your tracing to make all the hearts exactly alike. Instead, stitch one, then copy the second from the first and so on as if you were copying from a graph. Worked in this way, the hearts will cover the same number of canvas squares on all four sides and will be mirror images of each other.

A 10-gauge or gros point canvas would add texture, giving it a homespun, early American quality.

Colors
Bird: medium blue 733; wing: darker blue 723; beak and legs: yellow ochre 447; branch: brown 511; leaves: moss green 510; outer edge of hearts: dark red 810; scallops: white; middle hearts: pink 860; center hearts: red R10

Flowers in Vase

Don't be intimidated by the amount of detail in this design. It is challenging and some skill and time are required, but your patience will be rewarded by a gentle and graceful work.

Use as small a gauge canvas as you can without going into petit point.

A plain border or one with a tiny pattern would make an interesting frame.

Colors
Aqua in vase and flowers 773, orange in vase and flowers 424, yellow in vase and flowers Y44, pink in vase and flowers 649, rose in vase and flowers 821, bright light green G54, moss green 510, brick red in flowers 240, magenta 221

Chicken and Egg

Opposite

This is a perfect design for the beginning needle-pointer. It's easy, fun to do and works up very quickly. Any gauge canvas would be fine but we think a gros point would be most effective. A border in a solid color may be added, and the design would make a cheerful pillow or wall hanging for a child's room.

Colors
Chicken: golden yellow Y42; shading on chicken and chicken feet: brown 411; coxcomb and feet: red 242; egg and writing: white; sky: sky blue 743; ground: bright green G54

Woven Square

Page 62

At first glance this design looks quite complicated, but it is actually a good one for the needlepointer who has not yet tried a geometric or symmetric piece. The traced design may not look as even as the drawing, but once you start it is simply a matter of counting before it works itself into place. We suggest starting in the center square and working out from there. The diagonal thin lines on the left side will look smooth and the diagonal lines on the right side will look ragged as you work. But if you use the same number of stitches for the lines on each side, the finished piece will look symmetrical. Do not make the mistake of turning the design around as you do it. Remember to keep the canvas upright and work your stitches from right to left at all times. This one is best done on 12-gauge canvas.

Colors
Turquoise 763, dark orange 960, yellow 450, bright brick red 958, bright red R10, fuchsia 644

EGG

Instructions for this pattern appear on page 60.

Sun and Moon

Although the sun and moon designs can be worked separately, they are a natural pair and offer a number of possibilities as finished pieces. They would be especially exciting as a banner, but two pillows in a bedroom or a family room would certainly be both fun to work and to own. They are really perfect for any place a tandem design is desired.

Traced as is, the designs will be rather small. If you find this a problem, try placing them on a larger round or square background and finish the background with the same border that frames the faces themselves. In this way each of the designs or the design combination can be made as large as needed.

Any of the larger canvases are appropriate. A 10-gauge or gros point would work up very quickly, and if there are two needlepointers in the family the pair could be finished in no time at all.

Sun

Page 64

The perennial problem of what to outline comes up again in this design. Your own preference will make the decision. Everything in the face may be outlined, with only the eyes, mouth and cheeks another color. The eyebrow and nose pattern may be colored in a tone or two darker than the background of the face. The outline color can be bold —purple or navy or even red—or subtle, in browns, rusts or dark golds.

Colors
Entire background (face and frame): pale gold 442; nose, circle around cheeks, connecting line between cheeks and upper mouth: golden yellow Y40; cheeks, mouth, upper and under eyelids and inner rim of face: bright orange 960; iris, nostrils, design on top of scallops and polka dots: bright red R10; design on top of nose: medium gold 440; white of eye: white; scallops on frame: purple 642

Moon

Page 65

All the directions given for the Sun design work as well for the Moon with one exception. Because the face is next to a dark ground, no actual outlining is needed.

Think too about the border before you begin.

The possibilities of variation are less than those in the Sun design, but the stars can be worked in one color, alternating colors or many colors, and the Moon's profile can be anything from the purest white to the warmest golds.

Colors
Outside rim and inside stars: slate blue 330; stars in frame, left section of design, eyebrow and cheek: pale yellow 456; center profile: medium dusky purple 615; right section of design: pale dusky purple 620

Indian Landscape

The more complicated parts of this design are the borders and the detail of the trees. We stitched the solid color of the trees with a two-strand thread made of two different colors. This enabled us to achieve a leafy, mottled effect. The needlepoint has the look of a painting, so framing the finished product would be appropriate. It would also make a lovely pillow. The addition of initials or the date would make it an interesting commemorative gift.

Although our colors are naturalistic, if you prefer to fantasize a bit you could make the tree tops shades of the color of the room or make the main ground dark and the trees all jewel-like colors. It could be done in No. 10 canvas but since a larger mesh will make the detail of the trees hard to work out, a 12-gauge would be more suitable.

Colors
Red frame and berries 810, blue sky 322, large green background 550, green ground and tree 510, bright green G64, orange fruit 434, hot pink 821, brown ground stripe 134, light trunk 423, darker trunk 145, blue trunk 621

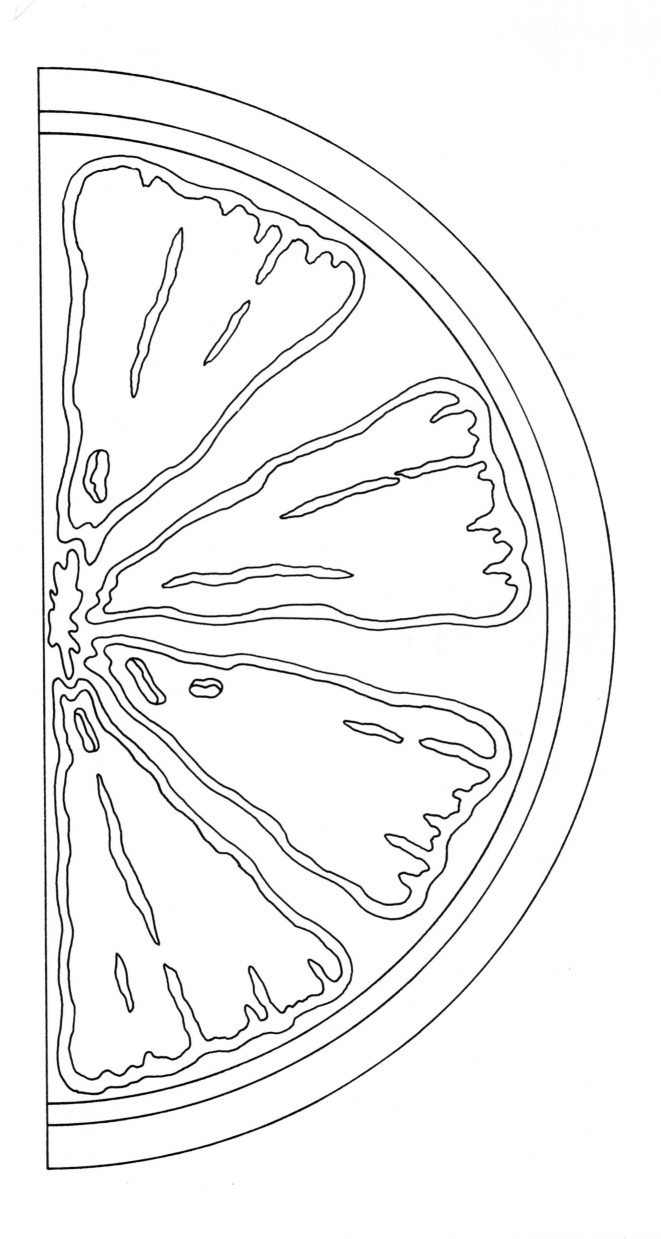

Citrus Half

Opposite

You can interpret this versatile design in a number of ways. Use the half slice as is, or make it a whole slice simply by turning the canvas around and tracing the half again. The design can be an orange, lemon, grapefruit or lime, whichever looks best in your room.

It can be stitched on any gauge canvas, but if you decide to do it in gros point, some of the detail might have to be eliminated.

It is not a difficult design to stitch, and a group of these pillows, both wholes and halves in all the citrus fruits, would be striking on a wicker couch or in a summer room.

Colors
Outer rind and lemon sections: yellow Y44; inner rind: burnt orange 424; seeds, outlines of sections and center design: white; shading of seeds: dark gray 162; background: citrus green 574

Indian Elephant

Page 70

This decorative elephant is for the advanced needlepointer. Many patterns are used on the same canvas so be sure to trace carefully. Where a pattern is repeated it is important to use the same number of stitches in each section so that the designs work out symmetrically. The piece should be done in canvas size No. 14, producing a jewel-like finished canvas.

Colors
Blue frame 773, green 510, yellow Y44, rose twist 821, light orange 434, dark orange 424, purple 623, hot pink 649, dark red 845

Cat in Window With Flowers

Page 71

Try framing this design or making it into a pillow for an antique rocker. It is an enchanting picture, and you will almost feel as if you are painting as you stitch. Use a 10-gauge or gros point canvas and work a flat-colored border around it as a frame to emphasize its pictorial quality.

Colors
Green background G54, orange cat 424, string, brown stripe and pot 414, yellow stripe Y44, red tulip 821, 639, blue tulip 773, 783, green tulip leaves and trees 555, 565, tree trunk 217, sky 773, frame 443

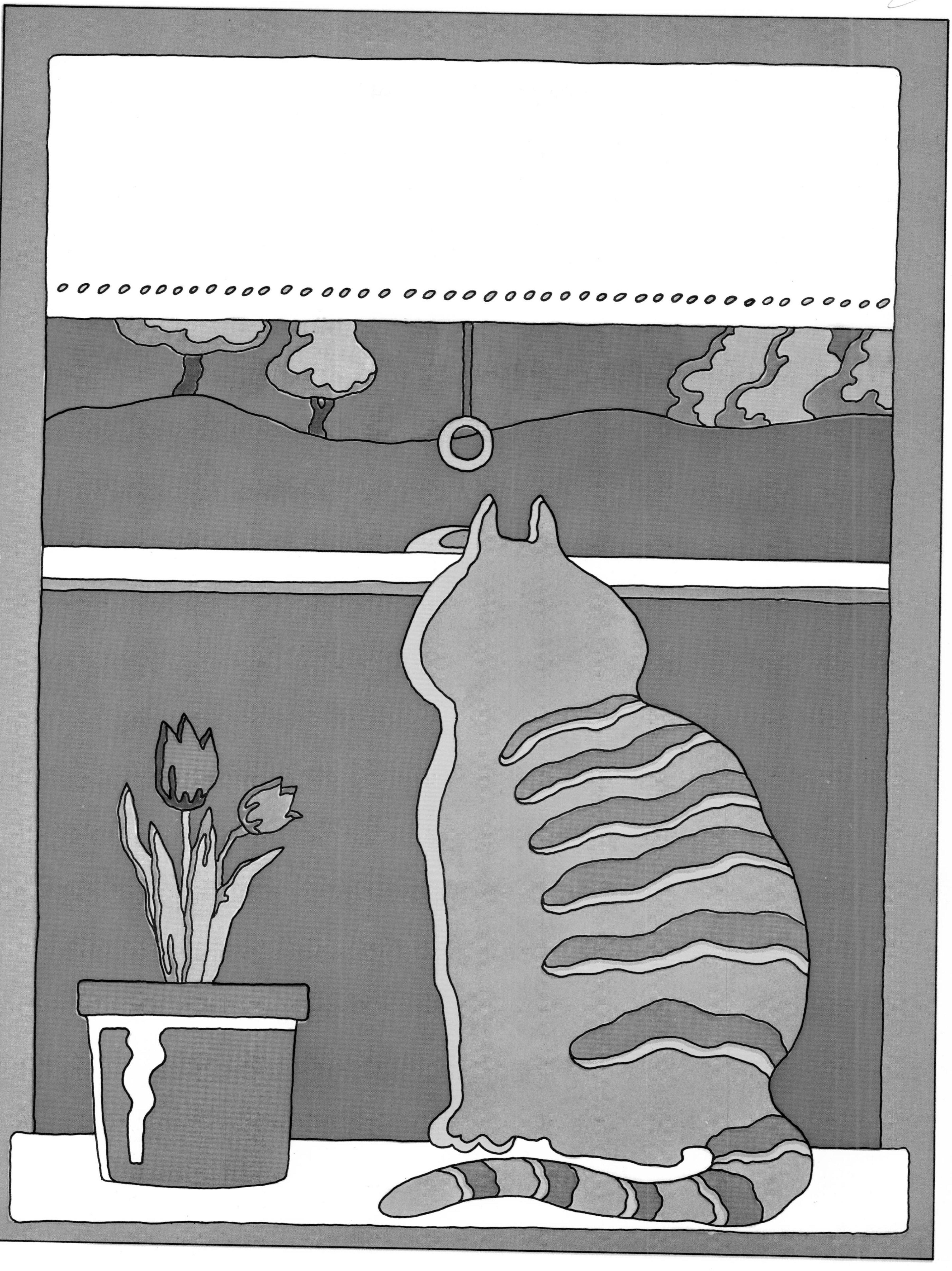

Tulip Quilt

Opposite

Adapted from an old quilting pattern, this design looks equally beautiful as a needlepoint. We have graphed half of it, and although it must be counted, it is not a difficult design to work.

When you have finished the half of the design that is graphed, simply turn the graphed design around and count out the other half. Start this design in the middle, doing the vines first and branching out to the leaves and tulips. Imagine there is a square in the center of the canvas and begin the vines from the corner of the square.

Colors
Center tulips: dark and light pinks 821, 827, 828; top corner tulips: dark and light purples 623, 653 with a highlight of pale pink 828; bottom corner tulips: warm reds 810, 850 with a highlight of medium purple 663; center branches attached to the center tulip: bright green G54; branches attached to bottom tulips: medium green 545; branches attached to top corner tulips: medium moss green 555; leaves: mixture of the same greens used on the branches

Oriental Medallion

Page 74

A design for the experienced needlepointer, although the novice might find it challenging and certainly workable with the help of the graph. As it is it would make a jewel-like pillow or beautiful evening purse, (use the design for both sides of the purse). The design may also be repeated for a rug on one large canvas or worked on a series of squares. It might be placed in the center of a canvas using a large background, or repeated as many times as needed for a piano bench or window seat.

Colors
Blue 773, red 242, orange 968, green 555, yellow Y44, gold Y40, magenta 221, coral R60

Cat on Rug

Page 75

Many of the animal enthusiasts we know might have fun stitching this design—a contented cat asleep on a rug. It is uncomplicated and can be worked even on gros point canvas with great effectiveness. A child might enjoy stitching it as a picture for her room or a pillow for her bed, and the novice will find it works up quickly and easily. It is a charming piece and could even incorporate your own cat's coloring and its name on a border.

Colors
Orange floor 965, dark floor stripe 414, tassels and rug 639, 821, blue rug 773, cat stripes Y40, Y44, pink nose 828, yarn 505, 555, blue features 334

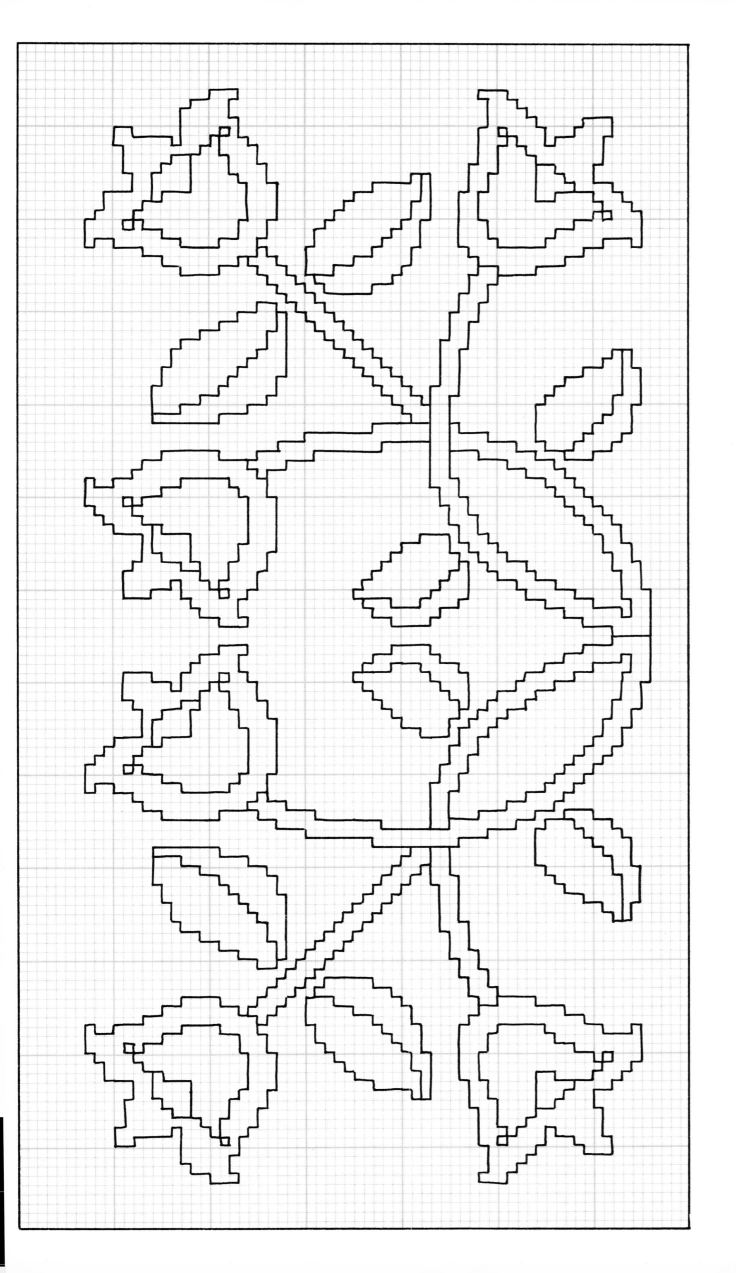

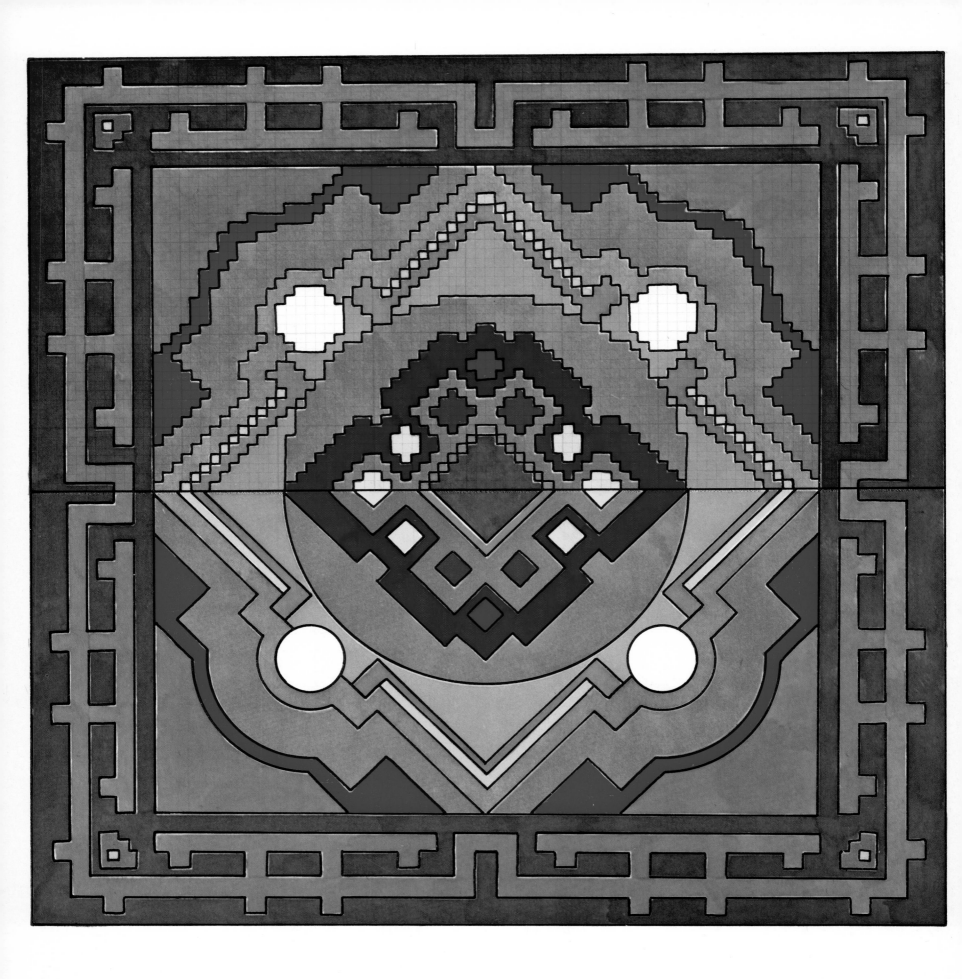

Plaid Strawberry

Opposite

This whimsical strawberry should be worked by a needlepointer who has had some experience, since it is important to line up the mesh of the canvas with the blocks of the design. This way you can easily follow the way the pattern works out evenly over the entire strawberry. You could do this needlepoint within a square frame but we think it would be far more effective to work the outline in the shape of the strawberry. This would make a fine pillow with the same design worked on the reverse to give you a novel three-dimensional stuffed fruit. If you are not so ambitious, a backing of green felt would carry out the theme nicely.

Colors
Background: pink fuchsia 649; lines of plaid: dark red 845; corner squares: dark fuchsia 639; center of squares: soft black 105; leaf: olive 555; shadow of leaf: bright green G54

Indian Rug Design

Page 78

The ambitious needlepointer can make this versatile design into a rug or an exciting set of cushions for chairs. Changing the colors can give the basic design different moods. Dark colors make it more sophisticated, lighter ones give it a gayer mood. The Indian rug design can also be used for a carryall bag. Do the needlepoint in the same colors or in contrasting colors on each side.

Colors
Dark blue 334, dark orange 968, dark green 510, gold Y40, brick red 242, hot pink 829, light yellow Y44

Great American Kiss

Page 79

What a wonderful wedding or anniversary gift this makes! It is an intriguing design, but look at it carefully before you begin. The profiles are actually repeated only three times. The other defining lines form a pattern that is not part of the faces, and it is important to realize this before you decide on your color scheme. This is also one of the few designs where the gauge of the canvas truly determines its effectiveness. A small mesh—No. 14 canvas—stresses the keen line of the profiles and lends a subtlety that would be lacking in a larger-mesh canvas.

Dates and names may be added in a border.

Colors
Background 773, red 240, orange 970, fuchsia 639

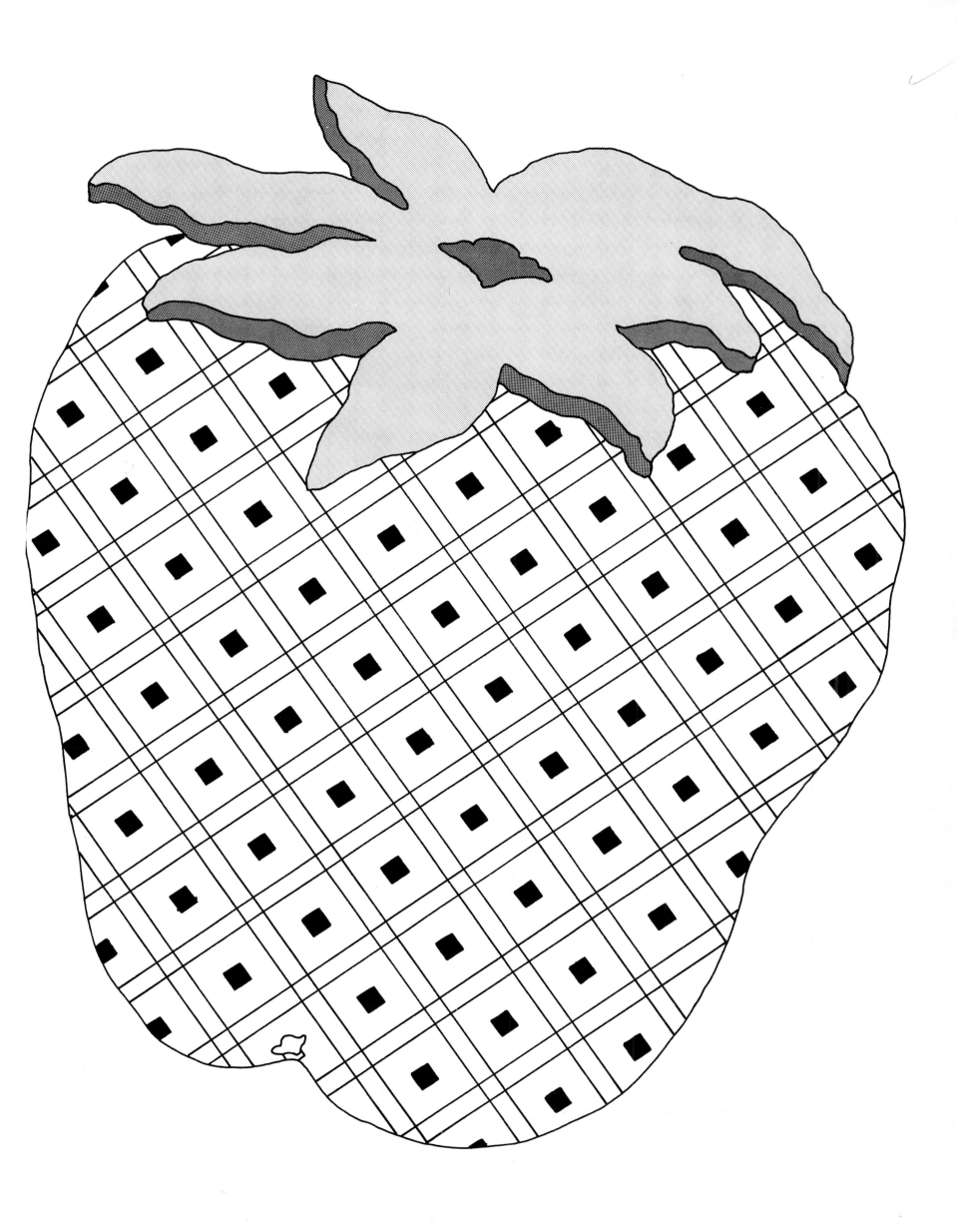

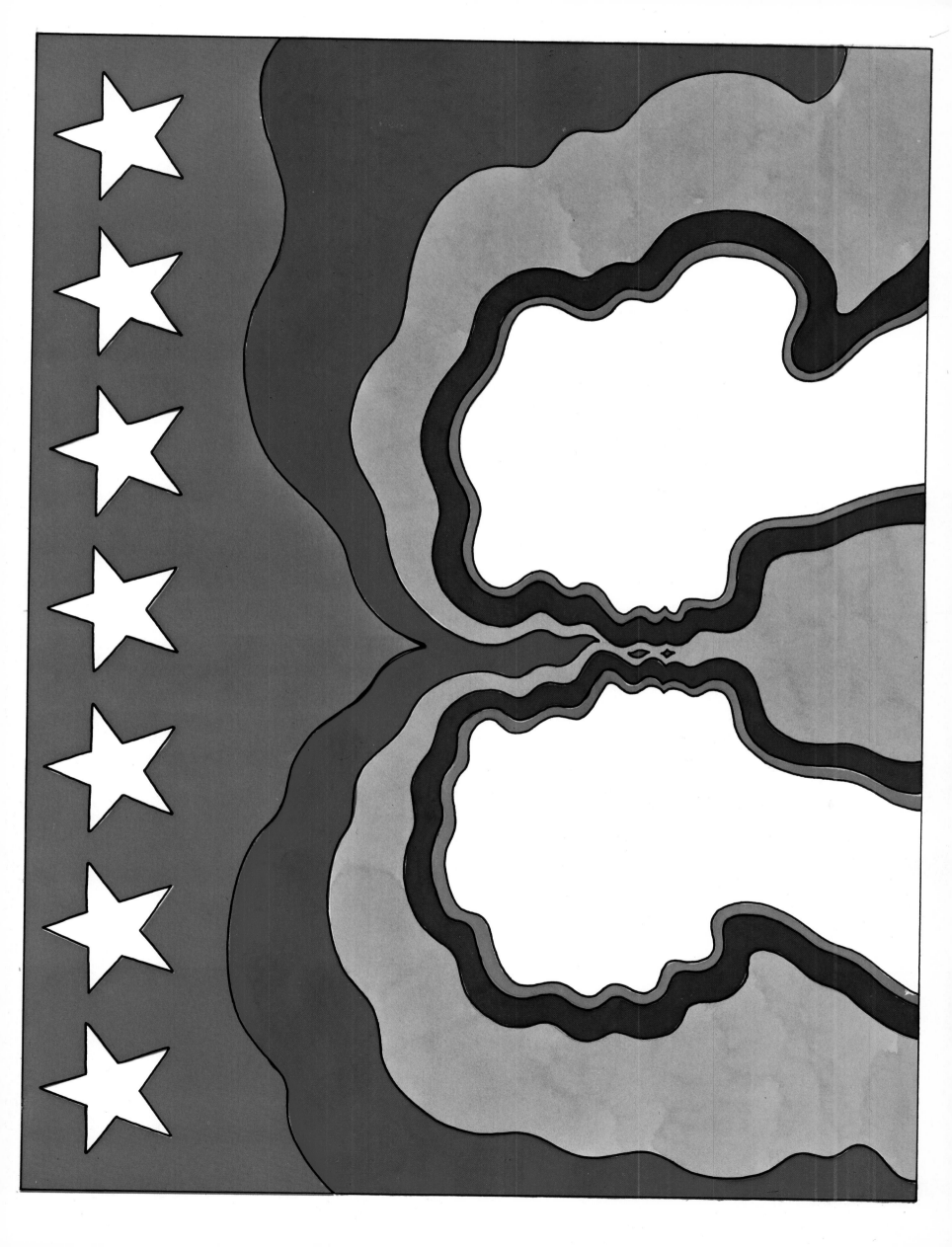

Water Lily

This Oriental pattern will intrigue the intermediate or advanced needlepointer. Since the theme requires a delicacy of line, one of the smaller-gauge canvases would set it off to its greatest advantage. The design is symmetrical so when you do the tracing be careful to line up both sides evenly on the canvas.

The design would make a beautiful pillow, and a plain border around it would enlarge, frame and give importance to the finished piece.

Colors
Background 127, gold 970, orange 958, darker orange 242, brick red R10, dark pink 821, light pink 288, purple 645

Folk Geometric

Opposite

You can work this lively design on any size canvas including gros point, although the smaller-gauge canvas you use, the more delicate the finished piece will appear. It makes an engaging picture or pillow but will also be effective framed under glass as a tray or covering a small parson's table or footstool. It is a bright and cheerful design and if you don't mind some counting, a pleasure to work.

Colors
Starting from the outside and working in, the corner design is: red R10, burnt orange 424, yellow 446, purple 642, red R10 (again) and yellow 446 (again). Background: dark turquoise blue 365; flowers: combinations of red R10, dark fuchsia 645, medium fuchsia 649, pink 659, and burnt orange 424; larger stems: light green G74, with shading of bright green G54; smaller stems in the center motif: bright green G54 with light green shading G74; geometric shape outlining the center design: yellow 446; background of the center design: white; larger center geometric figure: burnt orange 424; smaller center geometric figure: red R10; exact center: yellow 446

Astral Landscape

Page 84

The simple, dreamlike quality of this scene makes it an attractive design for the young beginning needlepointer. You can practice your stitches on the large grounds, while the wavy detail provides some interest. The stars will not all come out exactly alike but when the design is done, you will still have the effect of a starry sky. A 10-gauge canvas may be used.

Colors
Sky 318, yellow Y44, gray 164, reddish pink mountain 845, orange yellow Y40, purple 633, brick red R69, orange 958, green stripe G54, blue stripe 750, purple stripe 623, green hill 510

Still Life

Page 85

This easy design can be done either on a large- or small-gauge canvas, depending on the effect you wish to achieve. If you do it in gros point, the finished product (a pillow or framed wall hanging) would be most suitable for a study or child's room. If you decide to do it in smaller stitches, the finished needlepoint will be a more serious rendition of a pop art idea. This design would make exciting cushions for upholstered chairs in a kitchen or a vacation house, perhaps changing the color scheme on the checkerboard for each chair.

Colors
Fuchsia background and centers 644, gold flowers and napkin Y40, red flowers and stripe R50, dull green stems 555, bright green stem 574, turquoise glass stripes 773, aqua blue stripe and squares 748, gray 184, green plate G54

Adam and Eve

This primitive is for the advanced needlepointer. The canvas used should be at least 12-gauge or smaller since the figure detail will not work out well on a larger-size canvas.

The figures are naturally the more difficult part of the design and should be outlined for emphasis. We usually do not recommend black wool for outlining since it can be rather harsh. In this design, however, black might be very effective, giving the canvas the look of stained glass.

This design can be used for a pillow or a wall hanging. It will be fairly small, and a plain border would increase its size and add to its importance.

Colors
Background 741, Adam and Eve 437, hair, upper body outlines and feathers 144, Adam and Eve fig leaves, serpent's eye, apple stems, tree leaves 510, Eve fig leaf, grass, tree leaves G54, seats, lower body outlines, serpent outline 821, shading of seats, tree trunk 154, serpent, apple 242, serpent's eye 452

Japanese Oriole

The vivid coloring of this Oriental design makes it an especially exciting project. It is definitely for the advanced needlepointer, for it must be done in small-gauge canvas to incorporate all the detail. The transference of the pale flowers with their delicate branching must be done by an experienced hand. Our choice of colors follows the design's Oriental flavor but you could change the colors to your own taste or color scheme without changing the Japanese feeling. For example, a turquoise blue background with very pale pink flowers or a white background with pink or blue flowers would be beautiful. Don't change the bird, though, for its depth of color gives drama to the whole design.

Colors
Blue of bird 742, orange 242, fuchsia 821, gold Y40, bright green 510, dull green 530, kelly green 569, brown 131, gray 184, pink mouth 865

Gingham Apple

We tested this design on a novice needlepointer with great success. It is easy to trace and at the same time very interesting to do because it incorporates so many different patterns. It would be a lovely design for the young needlepointer to try in gros point as it works up quickly.

Colors
Apple: bright red R10; shadow on apple: dark red 810; background: bright yellow Y44; larger leaf, tear drop, reflection: dark moss green 505; smaller leaf: bright green G54; stem: light brown 411; shadow on stem: dark brown 104; dark gingham squares: royal blue 723; lighter gingham squares: medium blue 741

Tortoise and Water

Opposite
The linear sections of this design demand some skill in both tracing and needlepointing. Make sure you capture the differences between the striations on the separate sections of design where they appear. Keeping this in mind you will have a striking Japanese pillow.

Colors
Background 221, light green 545, dark green 521, green shading 520, outline of center turtle design G64, orange 968, dark blue 380, medium blue 386, light blue 395, yellow 467, gray 137

Alphabet

Page 94
Here is a basic, simple alphabet that can be used on any gauge canvas.

Borders

Pages 95 and 96

These designs work well as belts or as borders for other designs. They may also be used as borders around a canvas that bears the name and birth date of a child, or as a frame for a mirror or photograph. The backgrounds may be enlarged and all of the designs can be worked on any gauge canvas.

Page 95: Colors
Boats: background: medium bright blue 731; sails: white; boat: bright red R10; *Stars:* background: purple 642; stars: bright yellow Y44; *Birds:* background: pale aqua 765; birds: rose 231; shadow bottom of bird: dark rose 236; *Hearts:* background: white; hearts: red R10; *Elephants:* background: jade green 577; elephants: yellow Y44

Page 96: Colors
Ribbon: background 534, yellow Y44; *Cherry:* dark red R69, magenta 221, hot pink 649, dark green 545, light green 550; *Tulip:* background 510, hot pink 649, orange 424, yellow Y44; *Shaped Oval:* background 773, red 829, yellow Y44, orange 424; *Chain:* gold 427, blue shadow 765

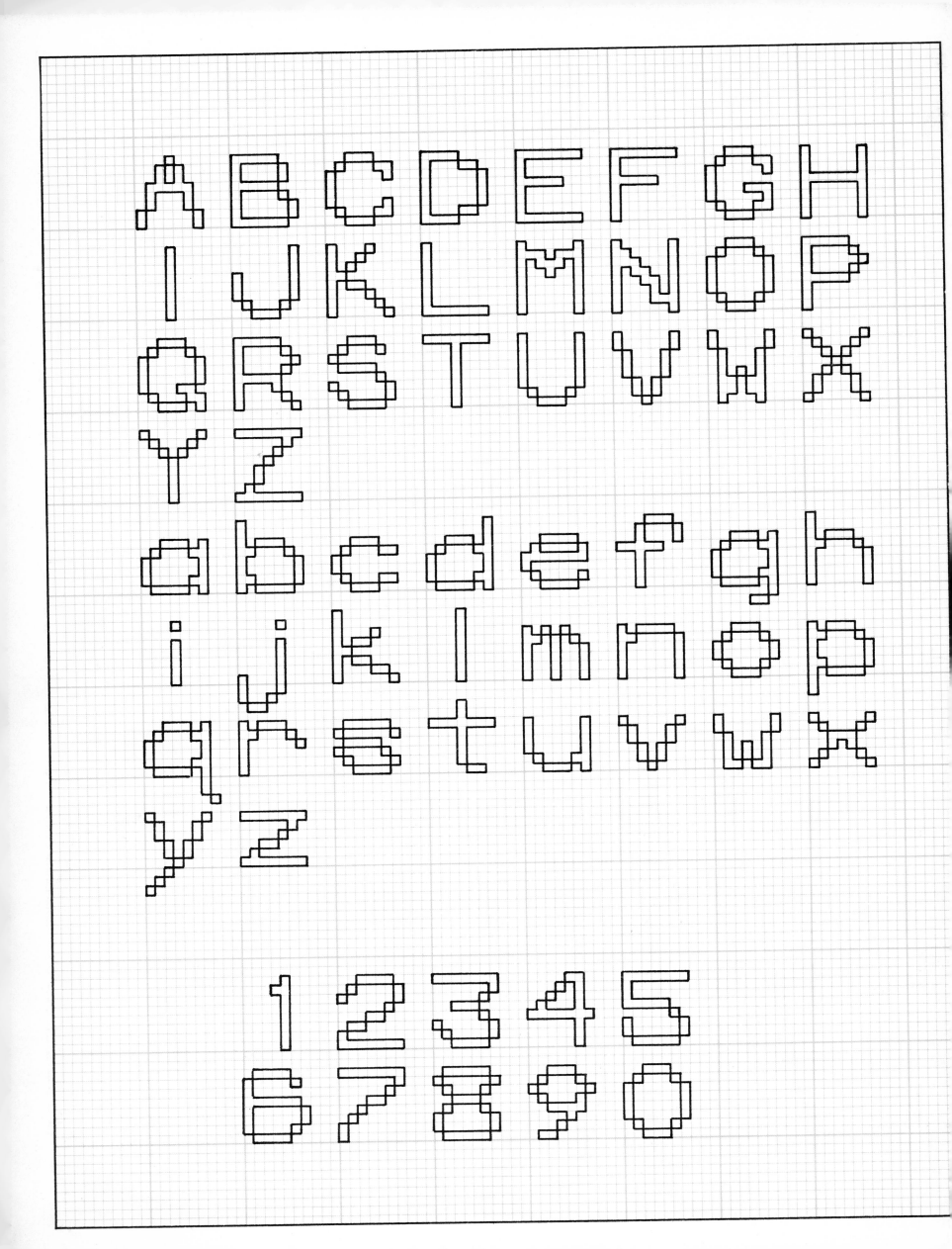

A B C D E F G H
I J K L M N O P
Q R S T U V W X
Y Z

a b c d e f g h
i j k l m n o p
q r s t u v w x
y z

1 2 3 4 5
6 7 8 9 0

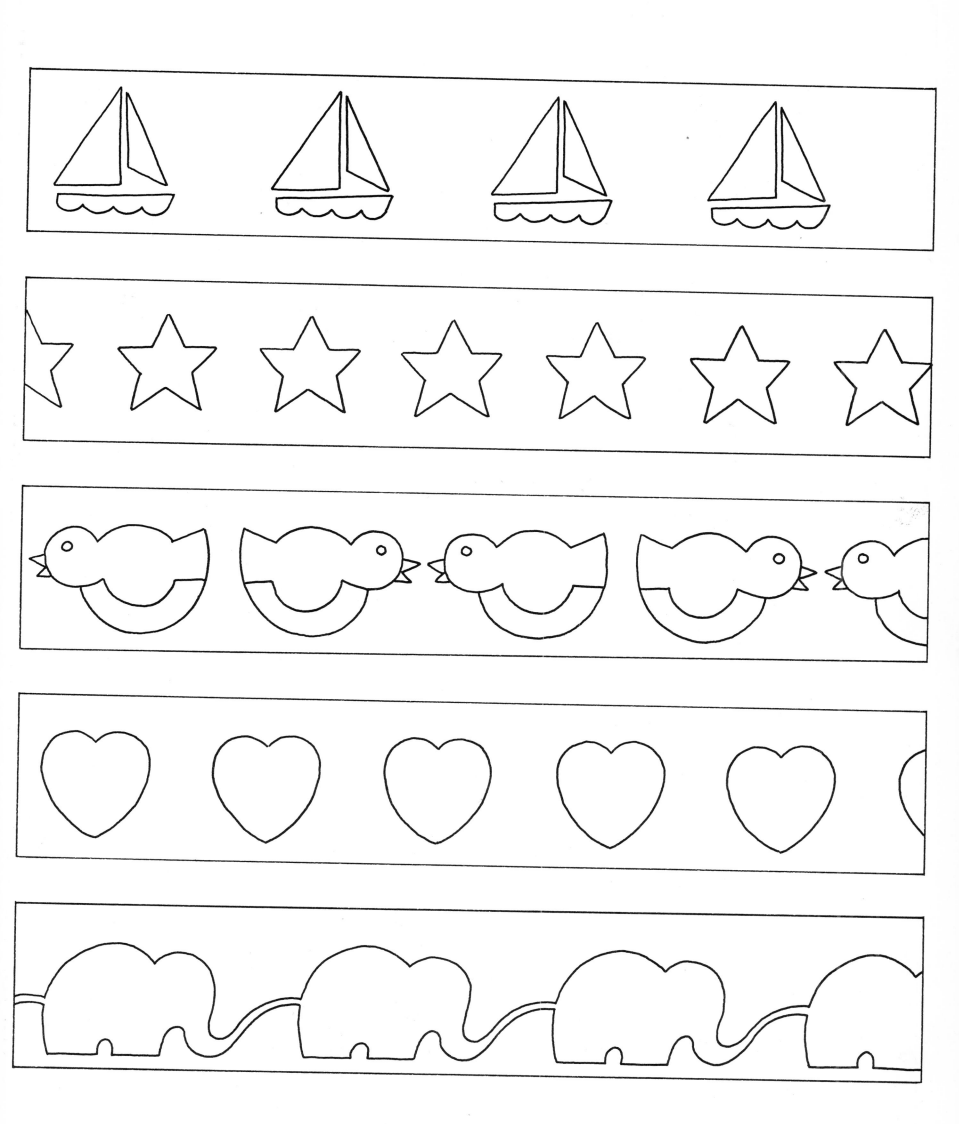